SCHOLASTIC

MATHS
SATs TESTS
YEAR 5

SCHOLASTIC

Book End, Range Road, Witney, Oxfordshire, OX29 0YD

www.scholastic.co.uk

© 2018 Scholastic Ltd

123456789   8901234567

A British Library Cataloguing-in-Publication Data
A catalogue record for this book is available from the
British Library.

ISBN 978-1407-18301-5
Printed and bound by Ashford Colour Press

Author and series editor

Paul Hollin

Editorial team

Rachel Morgan, Jenny Wilcox, Mark Walker,
Kate Baxter, Margaret Eaton, Julia Roberts

Illustrations

Tom Heard and Moreno Chiacchiera

Design

Nicolle Thomas, Alice Duggan
and Oxford Designers and Illustrators

Cover illustrations

Istock/calvindexter and Tomek.gr / Shutterstock/Visual Generation

Acknowledgements

Extracts from Department for Education website ©
Crown Copyright. Reproduced under the terms of the
Open Government Licence (OGL). www.nationalarchives.
gov.uk/doc/open-government-licence/version/3/

Every effort has been made to trace copyright holders
for the works reproduced in this publication, and the
publishers apologise or any inadvertent omissions.

Contents
Mathematics: Year 5

About this book

This book provides you with practice papers to help support children with end-of-year tests and to assess which skills need further development.

Using the practice papers

The practice papers in this book can be used as you would any other practice materials. The children need to be familiar with specific test-focused skills, such as ensuring equipment functions properly, leaving questions if they seem too difficult, working at a suitable pace for the tests and checking through their work.

If you choose to use the papers for revising content rather than practising tests do be aware of the time factor. These tests are short at only 30 or 40 minutes per paper, as they are testing the degree of competence children have.

Equipment

The following equipment will be needed for all test papers.

- pencil/black pen
- eraser

For papers 2 and 3 you may need:

- ruler (mm and cm)
- angle measurer / protractor

About the tests

Each maths test has three papers:

- Paper 1: arithmetic – these are context-free calculations. The children have 30 minutes to answer the questions. 40 marks are available.
- Paper 2 and Paper 3: reasoning – these are mathematical reasoning problems both in context and out of context. The children have 40 minutes per paper to answer the questions. 35 marks are available per paper.

The papers should be taken in order and children may have a break between papers. All of the tests broadly increase in difficulty as they progress, and it is not expected that all children will be able to answer all of the questions.

The marks available for each question are shown in the test paper next to each question and are also shown next to each answer in the mark scheme.

Advice for parents and carers

How this book will help

This book will support your child to get ready for the school-based end-of-year tests in maths. It provides valuable practice and help on the responses and content expected of Year 5 children aged 9–10 years.

In the weeks leading up to the school tests, your child may be given plenty of practice, revision and tips to give them the best possible chance to demonstrate their knowledge and understanding. It is helpful to try to practise outside of school and many children benefit from extra input. This pack will help your child to prepare and build their confidence.

In this book you will find two mathematics tests. The layout and format of each test closely matches those used in the National Tests so your child will become familiar with what to expect and get used to the style of the tests. There is a comprehensive answer section and guidance about how to mark the questions.

Tips

- Make sure that you allow your child to take the test in a quiet environment where they are not likely to be interrupted or distracted.
- Make sure your child has a flat surface to work on, with plenty of space to spread out and good light.
- Emphasise the importance of reading and re-reading a question.
- These tests are similar to the ones your child will take in May in Year 6 and they therefore give you a good idea of strengths and areas for development. When you have found areas that require some more practice, it is useful to go over these again and practise similar types of question with your child.
- Go through the tests again together, identify any gaps in learning and address any misconceptions or areas of misunderstanding. If you are unsure of anything yourself, then make an appointment to see your child's teacher who will be able to help and advise further.
- Practising little and often will enable your child to build up confidence and skills over a period of time.

Advice for children

- Revise and practise regularly.
- Spend some time each week practising.
- Focus on the areas you are least confident in to get better.
- Get a good night's sleep and eat a healthy breakfast.
- Be on time for school.
- Make sure you have all the things you need.
- Avoid stressful situations before a test.
- If a questions asks you to 'Show your method' then there will be marks if you get the method correct even if your answer is wrong.
- Leave out questions you do not understand and come back to them when you have completed those you can do.
- Check that you haven't missed any questions or pages out.
- Try to spend the last five minutes checking your work. Do your answers look about right?
- If you have time to spare and have a few questions unanswered, just have a go – you don't lose marks for trying.

Test coverage

The test content is divided into strands and sub-strands. These are listed, for each question, in a table at the end of every test to allow tracking of difficulties. In a small number of cases, where practical equipment such as containers would be required, these aspects are not tested.

Strand	Sub-strand
Number and place value	counting (in multiples)
	read, write, order and compare numbers
	place value; Roman numerals
	identify, represent and estimate; rounding
	negative numbers
	number problems
Addition, subtraction, multiplication and division (calculations)	add/subtract mentally
	add/subtract using written methods
	estimates, use inverses and check
	add/subtract to solve problems
	properties of number (multiples, factors, primes, squares and cubes)
	multiply/divide mentally
	multiply/divide using written methods
	solve problems (commutative, associative, distributive and all four operations)
Fractions	recognise, find, write, name and count fractions
	equivalent fractions
	compare and order fractions
	add/subtract fractions
	multiply/divide fractions
	fractions/decimals equivalence
	rounding decimals
	compare and order decimals
	multiply/divide decimals
	solve problems with fractions and decimals
	fractions/decimal/percentage equivalence
	solve problems with percentages

Strand	Sub-strand
Measurement	compare, describe and order measures
	estimate, measure and read scales
	money
	telling time, ordering time, duration and units of time
	convert between metric units
	convert metric/imperial
	perimeter, area
	volume
	solve problems (money; length; mass/weight; capacity/volume)
Geometry – properties of shape	recognise and name common shapes
	describe properties and classify shapes
	draw and make shapes and relate 2D and 3D shapes (including nets)
	angles – measuring and properties
Geometry – position and direction	patterns
	describe position, direction and movement
	coordinates
Statistics	interpret and represent data
	solve problems involving data

Instructions Test A: Paper 1

You **may not** use a calculator to answer any questions in this test.

Questions and answers

- You have **30 minutes** to complete this test.
- Work as quickly and carefully as you can.
- Put your answer in the box for each question.

- If you cannot do one of the questions, go on to the next one. You can come back to it later if you have time.
- If you finish before the end, go back and check your work.

Marks

- The number next to each box at the side of the page tells you the maximum number of marks for each question.
- In this test, short division and long multiplication questions are worth **2 marks** each. You will be awarded 2 marks for a correct answer.
- You may get 1 mark for showing a formal method.

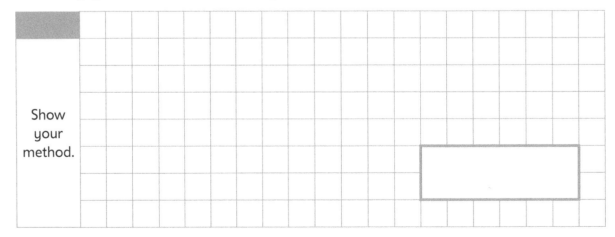

Show your method.

- All other questions are worth **1 mark** each.

Marks

1. 98 + 10 =

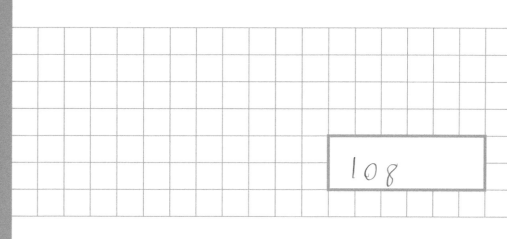

108

1

2. 4 × 5 =

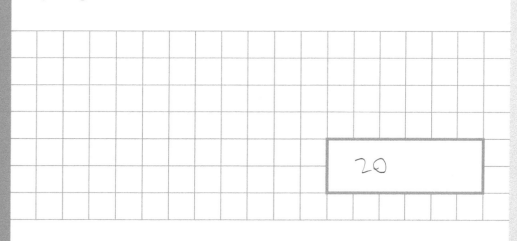

20

1

3. 37 + 52 =

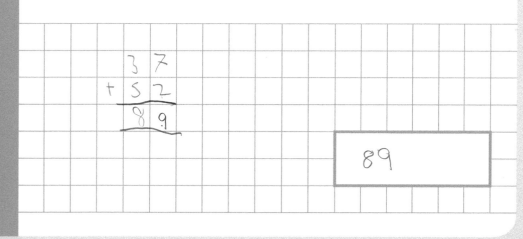

$$\begin{array}{r} 3\ 7 \\ +\ 5\ 2 \\ \hline 8\ 9 \\ \hline \end{array}$$

89

1

4. $0.8 - 0.6 =$

Marks

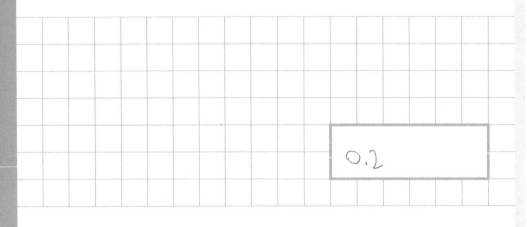

0.2

1

5. $63 - 19 =$

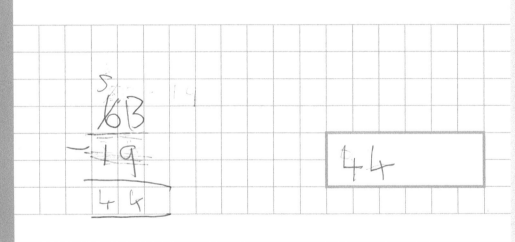

44

1

6. $87 \times 10 =$

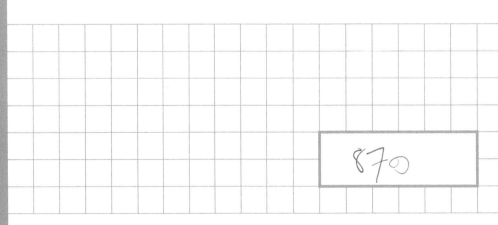

870

1

7. $45 \div 5 =$

9

Marks

1

8. $55 + 49 =$

104

1

9. $8 \times 12 =$

12 24 36 48 60 72 84 96

96

1

10. $\frac{2}{3} - \frac{1}{3} =$

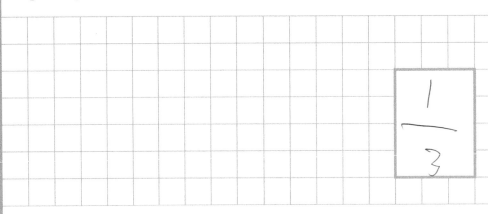

$$\frac{1}{3}$$

Marks

1

11. $0.6 + 0.3 =$

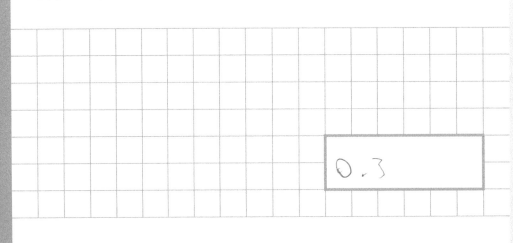

0.3

1

12. $5^2 =$

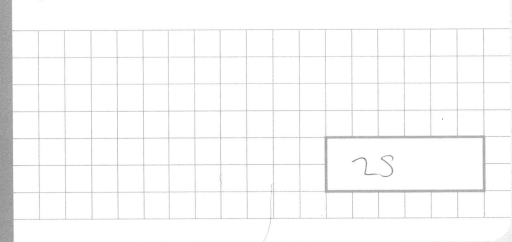

25

1

SCHOLASTIC National Curriculum SATs Tests

13. $90 \div 3 =$

1

14. $56.4 \times 10 =$

56.40

1

15. $\dfrac{1}{5} + \dfrac{1}{5} =$

$\dfrac{2}{5}$

1

16. $2000 - 200 =$

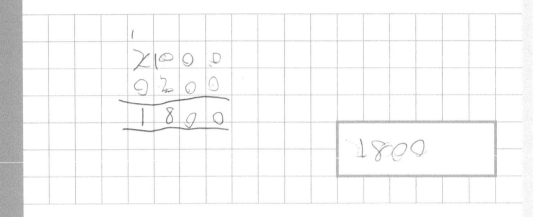

1800

Marks

1

17. $124 \div 4 =$

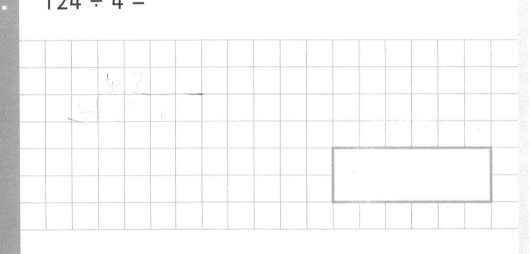

1

18. $628 + 380 =$

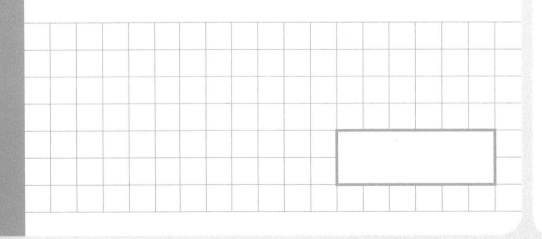

1

Marks

19. 2407 − 1552 =

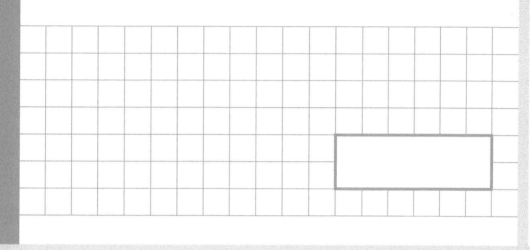

1

20. 115 ÷ 5 =

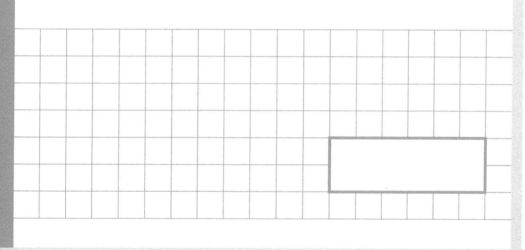

1

21. 23,412 − 3000 =

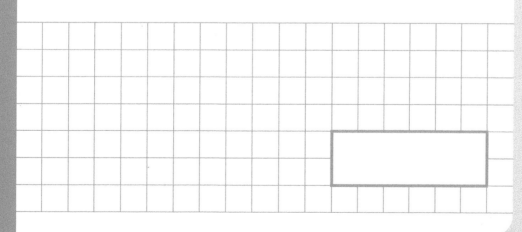

1

22. $3 + 7 - 3.5 =$

Marks

1

23. $\frac{1}{2} + \frac{1}{4} =$

1

24. $0.75 - 0.32 =$

1

SCHOLASTIC National Curriculum SATs Tests

25. 0.032 × 100 =

Marks

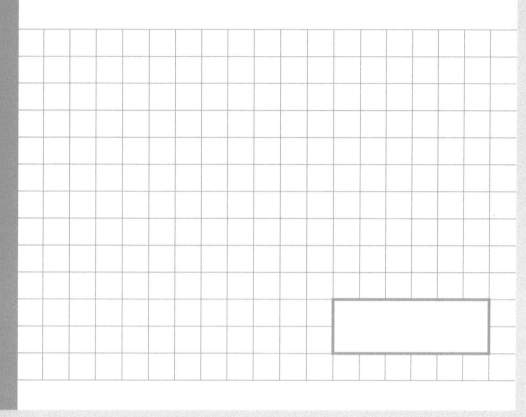

1

26.

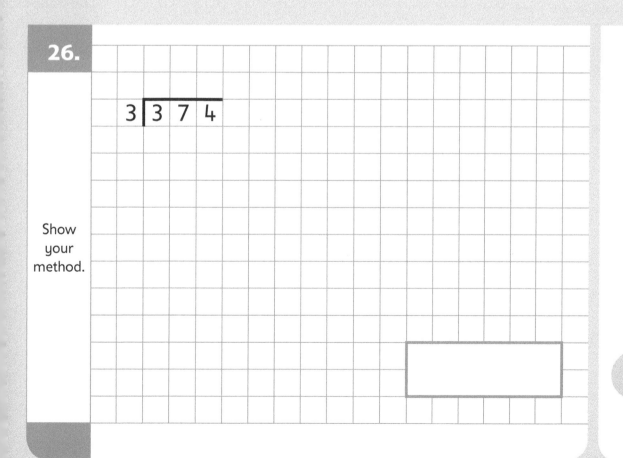

3) 3 7 4

Show your method.

2

Marks

27. $\frac{1}{4}$ of 24 =

1

28.

$$\begin{array}{r} 1\ 7\ 3 \\ \times\quad 4\ 2 \\ \hline \end{array}$$

Show your method.

2

29. 23,482 + 48,150 =

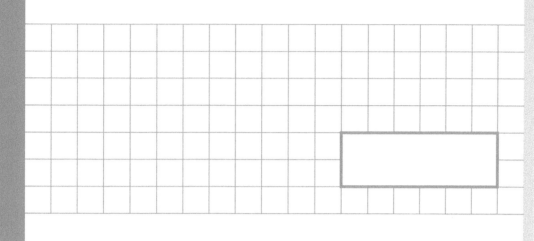

1

30. 35 × 30 =

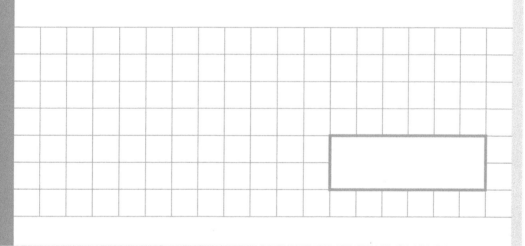

1

31. 2^3 =

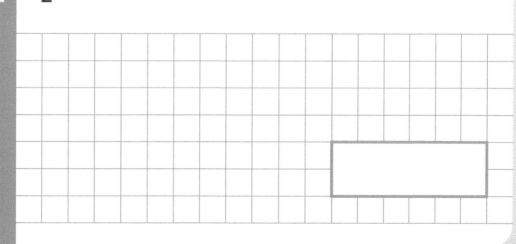

1

32.

Show your method.

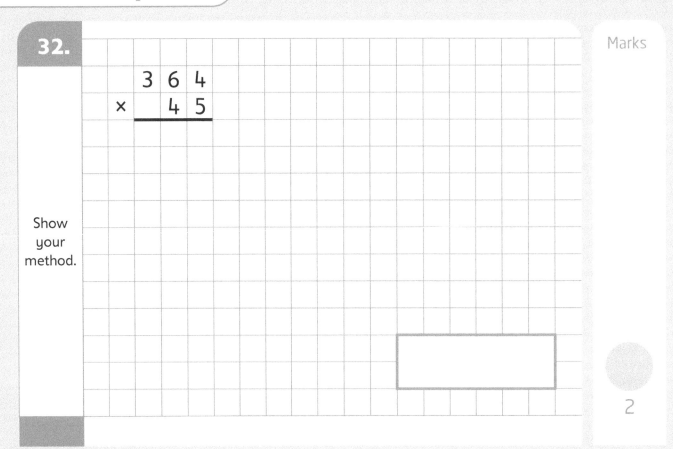

$$\begin{array}{r} 3\ 6\ 4 \\ \times\ \quad 4\ 5 \\ \hline \end{array}$$

Marks

2

33. $6 + 7 \times 5 =$

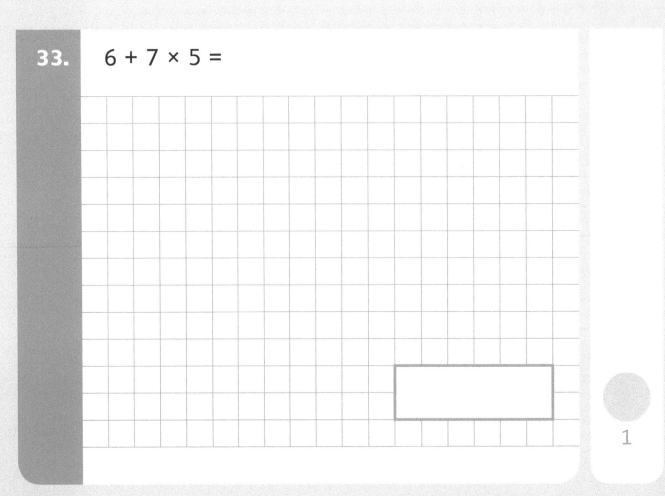

1

SCHOLASTIC National Curriculum SATs Tests

34.

Show your method.

$$7 \overline{)3\ 7\ 4\ 8}$$

Marks

2

35.

$63,462 \div 100 =$

1

36.

$\frac{3}{4} \times \frac{2}{3} =$

1

Test A: Paper 1 Marks

Q	Question	Possible marks	Actual marks
1	98 + 10	1	
2	4 × 5	1	
3	37 + 52	1	
4	0.8 − 0.6	1	
5	63 − 19	1	
6	87 × 10	1	
7	45 ÷ 5	1	
8	55 + 49	1	
9	8 × 12	1	
10	$\frac{2}{3} - \frac{1}{3}$	1	
11	0.6 + 0.3	1	
12	5^2	1	
13	90 ÷ 3	1	
14	56.4 × 10	1	
15	$\frac{1}{5} + \frac{1}{5}$	1	
16	2000 − 200	1	
17	124 ÷ 4	1	
18	628 + 380	1	

Q	Question	Possible marks	Actual marks
19	2407 − 1552	1	
20	115 ÷ 5	1	
21	23,412 − 3000	1	
22	3 + 7 − 3.5	1	
23	$\frac{1}{2} + \frac{1}{4}$	1	
24	0.75 − 0.32	1	
25	0.032 × 100	1	
26	$3\overline{)3\ 7\ 4}$	2	
27	$\frac{1}{4}$ of 24	1	
28	$\begin{array}{r} 1\ 7\ 3 \\ \times\ \ 4\ 2 \\ \hline \end{array}$	2	
29	23,482 + 48,150	1	
30	35 × 30	1	
31	2^3	1	
32	$\begin{array}{r} 3\ 6\ 4 \\ \times\ \ 4\ 5 \\ \hline \end{array}$	2	
33	6 + 7 × 5	1	
34	$7\overline{)3\ 7\ 4\ 8}$	2	
35	63,462 ÷ 100	1	
36	$\frac{3}{4} \times \frac{2}{3}$	1	
	Total	**40**	

SCHOLASTIC National Curriculum SATs Tests

Instructions Test A: Paper 2

- You have **40 minutes** for this test paper.

- You may **not use** a calculator to answer any questions in this test paper.

- Work as quickly and carefully as you can.

- Try to answer all the questions. If you cannot do one of the questions, **go on to the next one**. You can come back to it later, if you have time.

- If you finish before the end, **go back and check your work**.

- Ask your teacher if you are not sure what to do.

Follow the instructions for each question carefully.

If you need to do working out, you can use any space on the page – do not use rough paper.

Marks

Some questions have a method box like this.

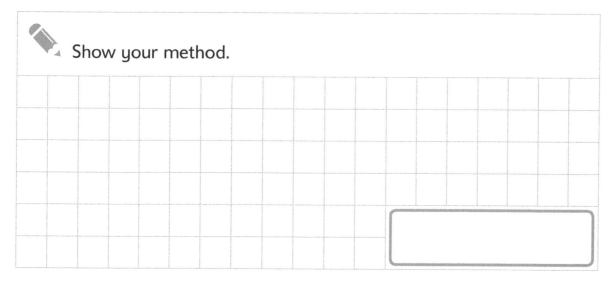

For these questions you may get a mark for showing your method.

The number on the right-hand side of the page tells you the maximum number of marks for each question.

1. Draw a circle around $\frac{2}{5}$ of the beads.

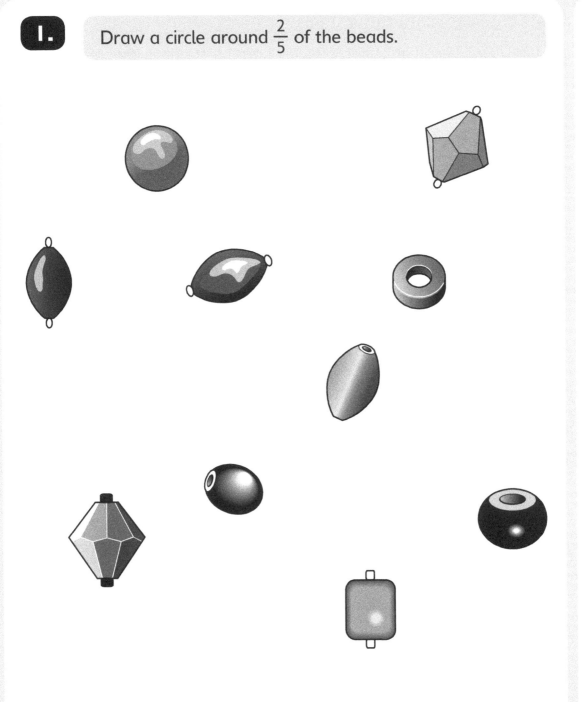

1

SCHOLASTIC National Curriculum SATs Test

2. Write the two missing digits to make this subtraction correct.

Marks

$$
\begin{array}{r}
4\ \square\ 2 \\
-\ 1\ 2\ \square \\
\hline
3\ 3\ 2 \\
\end{array}
$$

1

3. Mark −5°C on the thermometer.

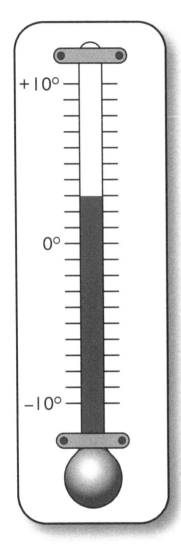

1

4. 245 x 7 =

Circle the correct answer.

1550

1612

1800

1715

Marks

1

5. Rashid rounds 835,455 to the nearest ten thousand.

Circle the correctly rounded number.

850,000   840,000   830,000   836,000   835,000

1

6. Round each of these decimals to the nearest whole number.

Marks

3.45 ☐

12.5 ☐

9.95 ☐

1

7. Write the missing numbers in this sequence.

943,506,   944,506,   ☐ ,   ☐ ,   947,506

1

8. Write 126 in Roman numerals.

Marks

1

9. How many centimetres are there in one kilometre?

Show your method.

cm

2

SCHOLASTIC National Curriculum SATs Tests

10. The population of a town is 14,675. If 9235 of the people are adults, how many children are there?

Marks

Show your method.

2

11. Draw a line to connect each shape to its correct name.

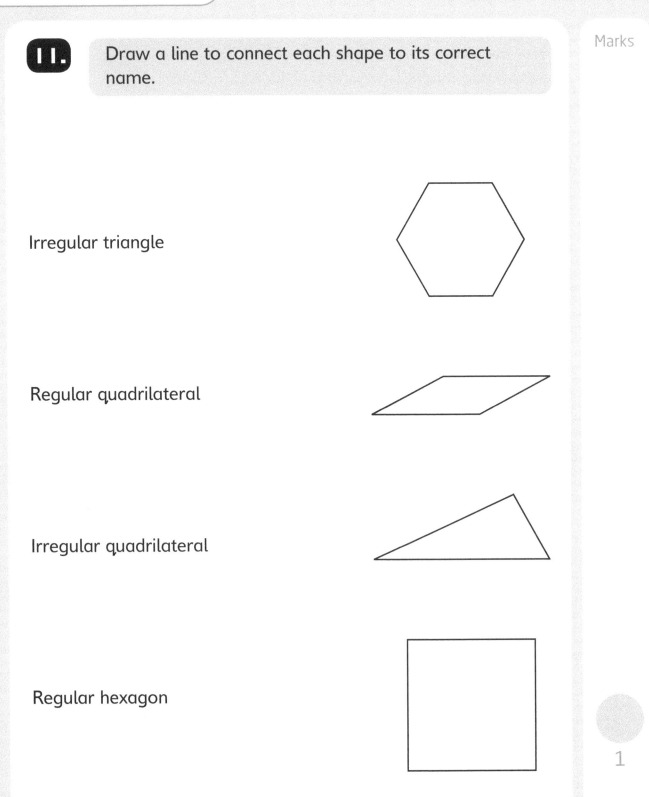

Irregular triangle

Regular quadrilateral

Irregular quadrilateral

Regular hexagon

1

SCHOLASTIC National Curriculum SATs Test

12. Complete the table. Write the fractions in their simplest form.

Marks

Fraction	Decimal	Percentage
		10%
	0.5	
$\frac{3}{4}$		
$\frac{1}{1}$	1.0	100%

1

13. The table shows the house points in a school at the end of the year.

There is a special school trip if the total is more than 5000.

House	Red	Blue	Yellow	Green
Points	1374	1685	989	1423

Will the children have a trip this year?

✎ Show your method.

2

14. Calculate each of these fractions.

Marks

$\frac{1}{2}$ of 56 = [   ]

1

$\frac{1}{4}$ of 60 = [   ]

1

$\frac{2}{3}$ of 27 = [   ]

1

Marks

15. Write all the factor pairs of 24.

1

16. The train journey from London Kings Cross to Newcastle usually takes two hours and twenty minutes.

The 11:30am train from Kings Cross leaves on time, but it is 25 minutes late on arrival.

What time does it arrive in Newcastle?

1

SCHOLASTIC National Curriculum SATs Tests

17. A theatre has three seating areas.

Zone B
180 seats, £33 each

Zone C1
50 seats,
£22.50 each

Zone A
120 seats, £39 each

Zone C2
50 seats,
£22.50 each

Marks

Estimate to the nearest £1000 how much money would be taken at the box office if every ticket was sold.

£

1

Calculate exactly how much money would be made from selling all the seats in **Zone A**.

Show your method.

2

Marks

18. Reflect the shape ABC in the dotted line.

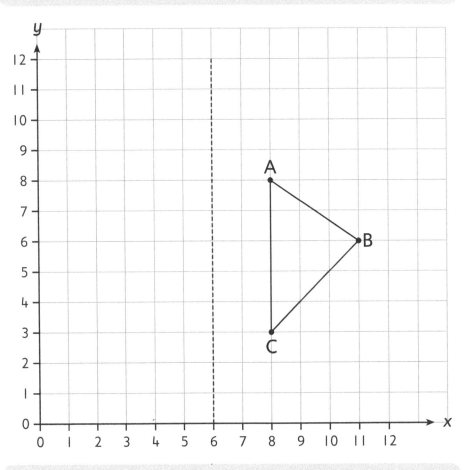

Write the coordinates for the new shape.

1

A reflected: (_____ , _____)

B reflected: (_____ , _____)

C reflected: (_____ , _____)

1

What do you notice about the reflected coordinates?

_____

_____

1

19. The bar chart shows transport to school for 50 children.

Draw the bar for **bus**.

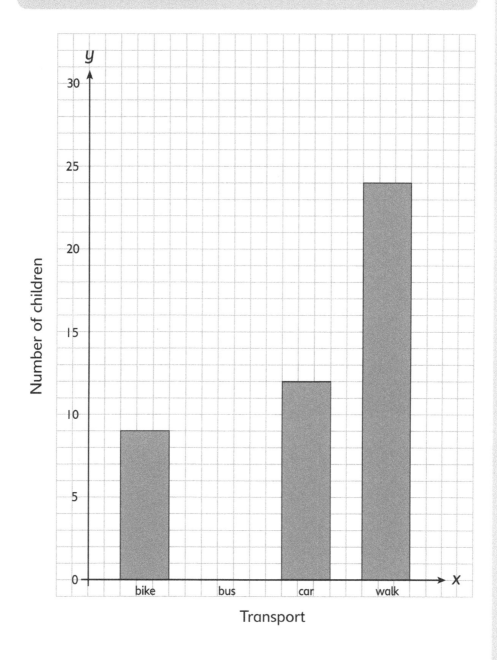

Complete this sentence.

Twice as many children _____

to school than travel by _____.

1

1

20. Tim says 6489 plus 12,857 equals 19,346.

Use an inverse calculation to prove that Tim is right.

1

■SCHOLASTIC National Curriculum SATs Tests

21. Some children make cupcakes to sell at the school fair for charity.

Marks

50 cases 75p

cakes 8p each

toppings 2p each

If they make 50 cakes and then sell them for 25p each, calculate how much profit they will make.

✏ Show your method.

2

22. Circle the fraction which, when multiplied by 4, will give a whole number.

$$\frac{25}{75}$$

$$\frac{45}{180}$$

$$\frac{35}{100}$$

$$\frac{55}{200}$$

1

SCHOLASTIC National Curriculum SATs Tests

23. The players on a five-a-side football team receive a bonus payment for winning a game. £1795 is shared between the five players.

How much will each player receive?

Show your method.

£

2

Test A: Paper 2 Marks

Q	Strand	Sub-strand	Possible marks	Actual marks
1	Fractions, decimals, %	Recognise, find, write, name and count fractions	1	
2	Calculations	Add / subtract mentally	1	
3	Number and place value	Negative numbers	1	
4	Calculations	Multiply / divide using written methods	1	
5	Number and place value	Identify, represent and estimate; rounding	1	
6	Fractions, decimals, %	Rounding decimals	1	
7	Number and place value	Counting (in multiples)	1	
8	Number and place value	Place value; Roman numerals	1	
9	Measurement	Convert between metric units	2	
10	Calculations	Add / subtract using written methods	2	
11	Geometry – properties of shapes	Describe properties and classify shapes	1	
12	Fractions, decimals, %	Fractions / decimal / percentage equivalence	1	
13	Calculations	Add / subtract to solve problems	2	
14	Fractions, decimals, %	Multiply / divide fractions	3	
15	Calculations	Properties of number (factors)	1	
16	Measurement	Telling time, ordering time, duration and units of time	1	
17	Number and place value	Number problems	3	
18	Geometry – properties of shapes	Describe position, direction and movement	3	
19	Statistics	Interpret and represent data	2	
20	Calculations	Estimate, use inverses and check	1	
21	Measurement	Money	2	
22	Fractions, decimals, %	Multiply / divide fractions	1	
23	Calculations	Multiply / divide using written methods	2	
		Total	**35**	

■SCHOLASTIC National Curriculum SATs Tests

Instructions Test A: Paper 3

- You have **40 minutes** for this test paper.
- You may **not use** a calculator to answer any questions in this test paper.
- Work as quickly and carefully as you can.
- Try to answer all the questions. If you cannot do one of the questions, **go on to the next one**. You can come back to it later, if you have time.
- If you finish before the end, **go back and check your work**.
- Ask your teacher if you are not sure what to do.

Follow the instructions for each question carefully.

If you need to do working out, you can use any space on the page – do not use rough paper.

Marks

Some questions have a method box like this.

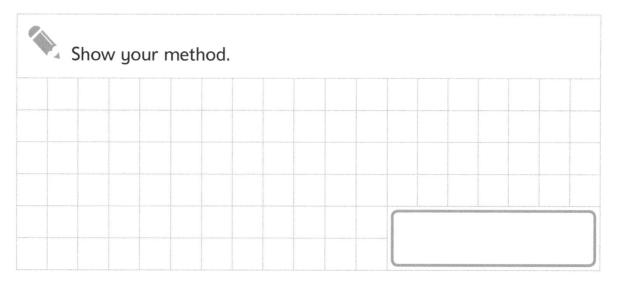

Show your method.

For these questions you may get a mark for showing your method.

The number on the right-hand side of the page tells you the maximum number of marks for each question.

1. Draw a line of symmetry on each of these shapes.

Marks

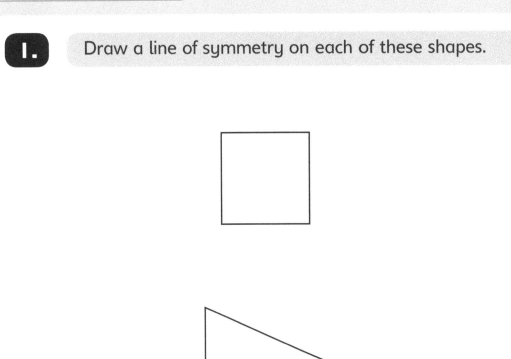

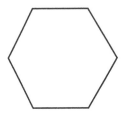

1

Marks

2. Draw lines from each decimal to the correct place on the number line.

1.25   1.5   1.95

1 |__|__|__|__|__|__|__|__|__|__|__| 2

1

3. Complete the sequence.

25,   50,   75,   [   ] ,   [   ] ,   [   ]

1

4. Is 2480 × 11 greater than 25,000? Write yes or no in the box.

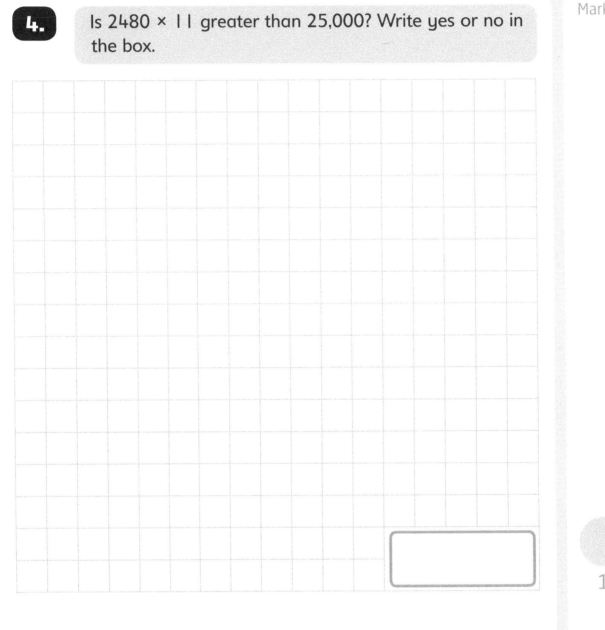

Marks

1

5. The temperature at noon is 12°C. At midnight the temperature is −5°C.

How many degrees has the temperature fallen by?

Marks

°C

1

6. Draw lines to match each fraction to its decimal equivalent.

Marks

$\frac{1}{8}$
$\frac{3}{10}$
$\frac{41}{100}$
$\frac{1}{2}$
$\frac{3}{4}$

0.5
0.41
0.125
0.75
0.3

1

7. There are 240 children in a school. The head teacher needs to order new resources. She orders one of each item per child.

stationary catalogue

ruler: 14p   pen: 12p   pencil: 8p   eraser: 5p

How much will the total order cost?

Show your method.

£

2

The cost for 100 exercise books is £32.

What is the cost per book?

p

1

8. Write this number in words: 463,901.

Marks

_____

_____

1

Write this number in digits.

seven hundred and four thousand, and twenty

1

Marks

9. These are the results for a class survey of pet ownership.

Pet	Dog	Cat	Guinea pig	Other pets	No pet
Number in class	7	8	4	6	5

Draw a bar chart to show the results of the survey.

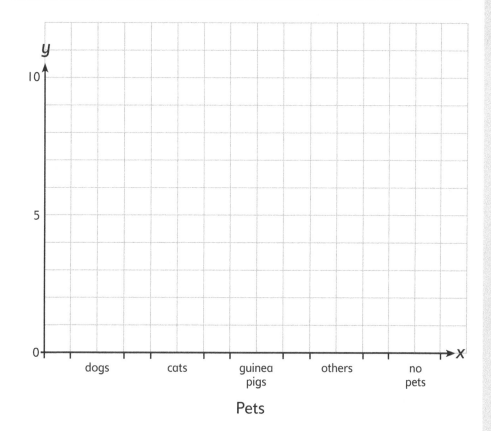

2

What fraction of the class has no pet?

Give your answer in its simplest form.

1

Marks

10. Jasper bakes a cake.

Jasper eats $\frac{1}{4}$ of it, his brother eats $\frac{1}{6}$ of it and his dog eats $\frac{1}{2}$ of it!

How much of the cake is left?

✎ Show your method.

2

SCHOLASTIC National Curriculum SATs Tests

Marks

11. There are 458 children in a large primary school.

If there are 179 in KS1, how many children are in KS2?

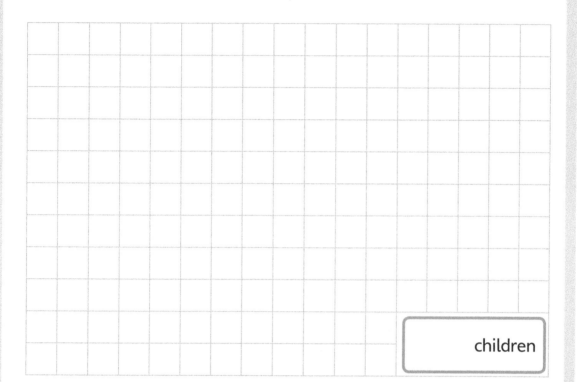

children

1

12. Write these decimals in increasing order, from smallest to largest.

0.105   0.510   0.501   0.051   0.150   0.015

1

13. Insert these signs in the correct boxes to make this calculation correct.

Marks

+   −   ÷

45 ☐ 9 ☐ 53 ☐ 32 = 26

1

■SCHOLASTIC National Curriculum SATs Test

Marks

14. How many degrees does a clock hand have to rotate to get from 12 to 9?

1

What is the name of this angle?

1

Marks

15. XC − XXIII =

Give your answer in Roman numerals.

1

16. Becky goes to the cinema with her little brother and her mum.

They share one box of popcorn.

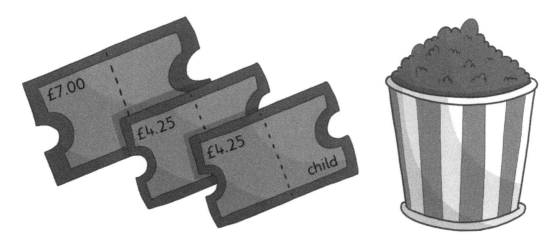

Becky's mum pays with a £20 note and received £2 change.

How much was the popcorn?

✏️ Show your method.

£

2

Marks

17. A city has a population of 254,346.

If 132,417 people are female, how many are male?

1

18. 147 grapes are shared equally between 12 children.

How many grapes are left over?

grapes

1

19. Nine rectangular tables are arranged in a group, as shown below.

Marks

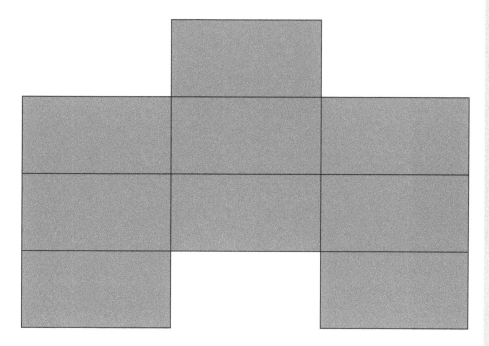

If each table is 1.5m long and 1m wide, calculate the perimeter and area of the group.

✏️ Show your method.

Perimeter

_____ m

Area

_____ m²

2

20. A family are buying an apartment for £156,000.
They pay a deposit of £50,000.

How much do they still owe?

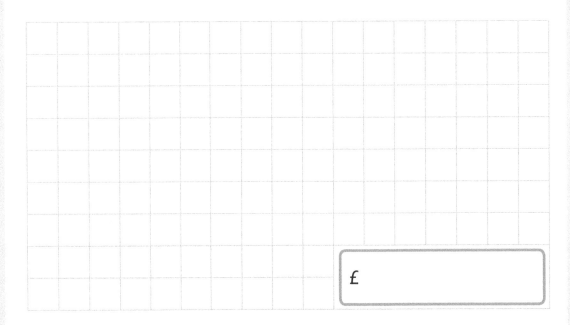

£

Marks

1

21.

The graph shows the change in temperature over a 10-hour period.

Marks

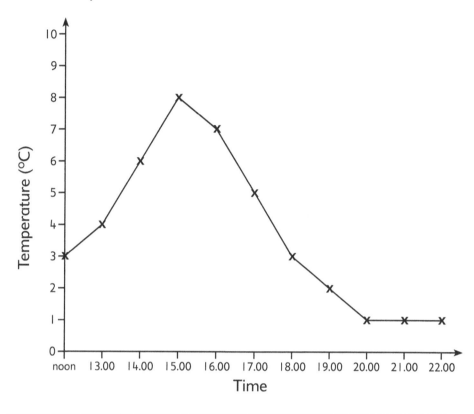

At what time did the temperature reach its lowest point?

1

What is the difference between the highest and lowest temperatures?

°C

1

How long was there between the two occasions when the temperature was 6°C?

1

22. 2760 people go to a football match.

$\frac{1}{2}$ of the people support the blue team.

$\frac{3}{5}$ of the blue supporters are wearing scarves.

How many blue supporters are not wearing scarves?

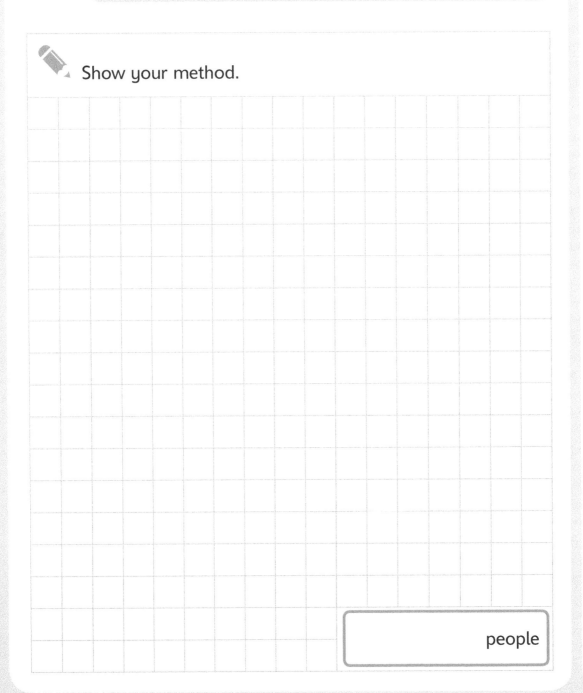

Show your method.

people

3

SCHOLASTIC National Curriculum SATs Tests

Q	Strand	Sub-strand	Possible marks	Actual marks
1	Geometry – properties of shapes	Describe properties and classify shapes	1	
2	Fractions, decimals, %	Compare and order decimals	1	
3	Number and place value	Counting (in multiples)	1	
4	Calculations	Estimate, use inverses and check	1	
5	Number and place value	Number problems	1	
6	Fractions, decimals, %	Fractions / decimals equivalence	1	
7	Calculations	Multiply / divide using written methods	3	
8	Number and place value	Read, write, order and compare numbers	2	
9	Statistics	Interpret and represent data	3	
10	Fractions, decimals, %	Add / subtract fractions	2	
11	Calculations	Add / subtract using written methods	1	
12	Fractions, decimals, %	Compare and order decimals	1	
13	Calculations	Order of operations	1	
14	Geometry – properties of shapes	Angles – measuring and properties	2	
15	Number and place value	Place value; Roman numerals	1	
16	Measurement	Money problem	2	
17	Calculations	Add / subtract to solve problems	1	
18	Calculations	Multiply / divide mentally	1	
19	Measurement	Perimeter, area	2	
20	Number and place value	Place value	1	
21	Statistics	Solve problems involving data	3	
22	Fractions, decimals, %	Multiply / divide fractions	3	
		Total	35	

Instructions Test B: Paper 1

You **may not** use a calculator to answer any questions in this test.

Questions and answers

- You have **30 minutes** to complete this test.
- Work as quickly and carefully as you can.
- Put your answer in the box for each question.

- If you cannot do one of the questions, **go on to the next one**. You can come back to it later if you have time.
- If you finish before the end, **go back and check your work**.

Marks

- The number next to each box at the side of the page tells you the maximum number of marks for each question.
- In this test, short division and long multiplication questions are worth **2 marks** each. You will be awarded 2 marks for a correct answer.
- You may get 1 mark for showing a formal method.

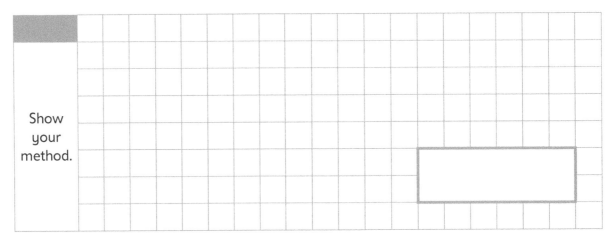

Show
your
method.

- All other questions are worth **1 mark** each.

SCHOLASTIC National Curriculum SATs Tests

Marks

1. 6 + 0.3 =

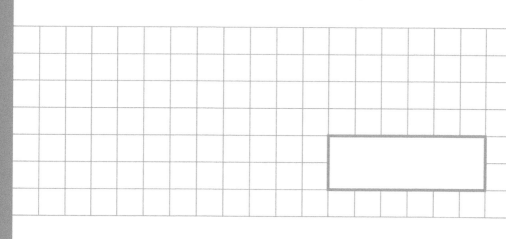

1

2. 8 × 3 =

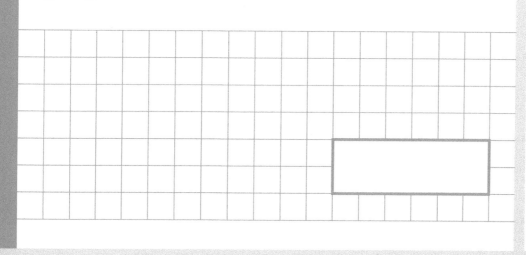

1

3. 12 + 6 + 9 + 14 =

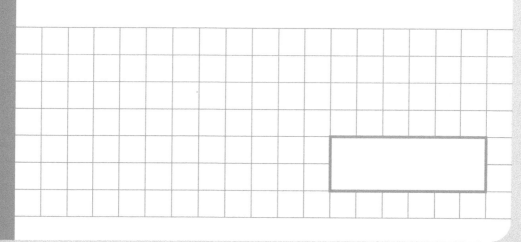

1

Marks

4. $\frac{1}{4} + \frac{1}{4} + \frac{1}{4} =$

1

5. $1473 - 73 =$

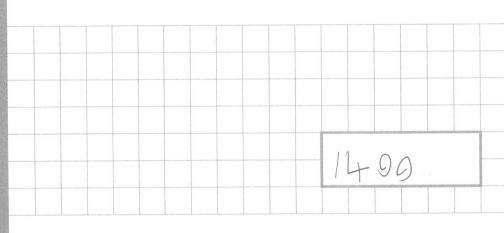

1

6. $25 \div 5 =$

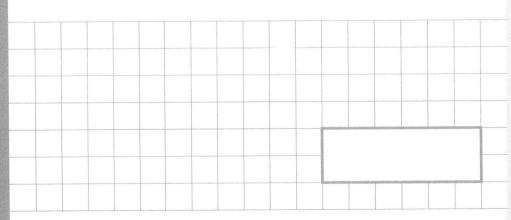

1

■SCHOLASTIC National Curriculum SATs Test

7.   475 + 98 =

Marks

1

8.   100 × 16 =

1

9.   2 × 3 × 4 =

1

10. $1000 \div 10 =$

Marks

1

11. $\frac{1}{12} + \frac{10}{12} =$

1

12. $1.25 \times 10 =$

1

13. 846,248 + 50,000 =

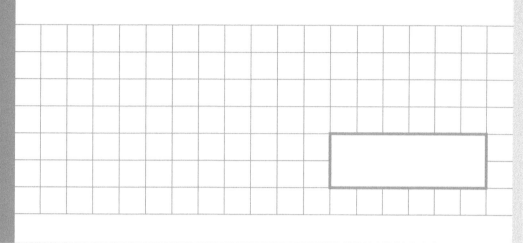

1

14. 0.77 − 0.25 =

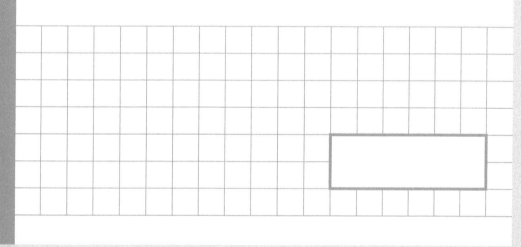

1

15. 23 × 9 =

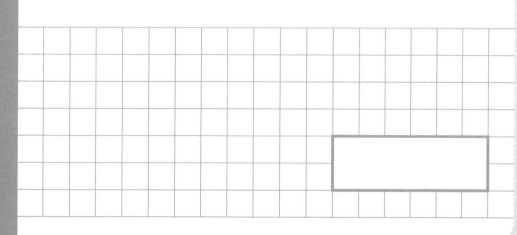

1

16. $0.2 + 0.9 =$

1

17. $\frac{1}{2}$ of 26 =

1

18. $387 - 222 =$

1

SCHOLASTIC National Curriculum SATs Test

19. $345 \div 100 =$

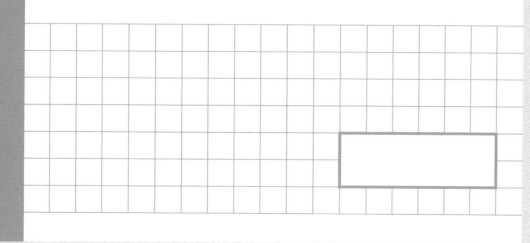

Marks

1

20. $7 + 4 \times 6 - 3 =$

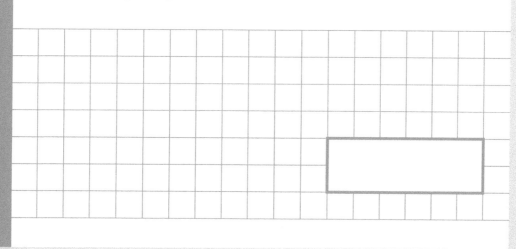

1

21. $12,385 + 28,034 =$

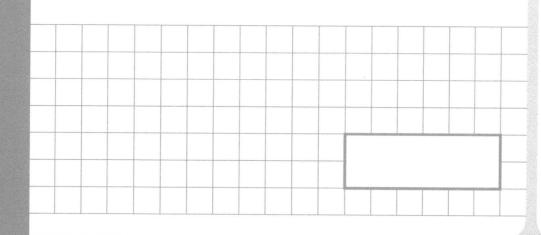

1

22. $35 \times 40 =$

1

23. $44 \times 11 =$

1

24. $1 - 0.65 =$

1

25. 32,406 − 16,273 =

Marks

1

26. 50% of 80 =

1

27.

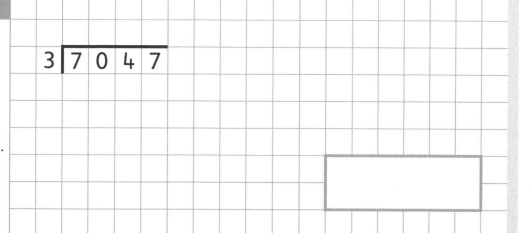

3 | 7 0 4 7

Show your method.

2

28. 15,634 − 3996 =

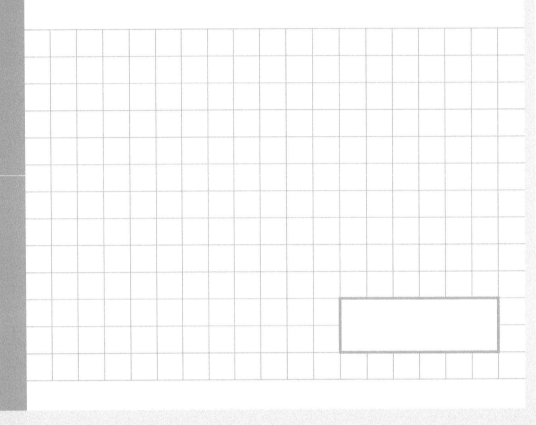

Marks

1

29. 87 × 53 =

Show your method.

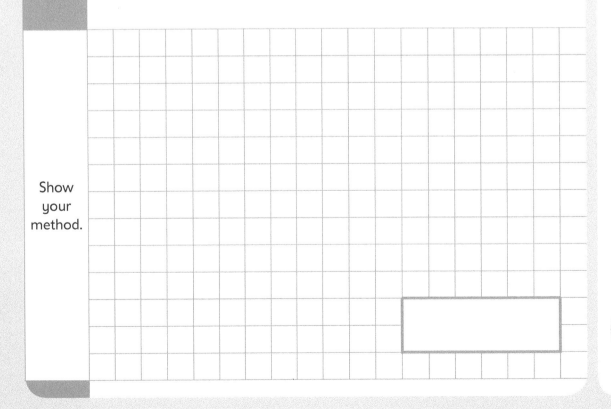

2

■SCHOLASTIC National Curriculum SATs Tests

Marks

30. $\dfrac{5}{8} - \dfrac{1}{2} =$

1

31. $30 + 3 \times 7 =$

1

32. $315 \times 34 =$

Show your method.

Marks

2

33. $1.75 + 2.16 =$

1

Marks

34.

$3 \times 1\frac{1}{2} =$

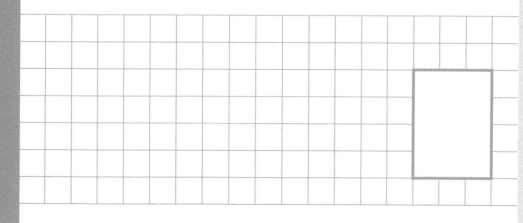

1

35.

Show your method.

$6\,\overline{)4\ 8\ 2\ 5}$

2

36.

$\frac{1}{3} + \frac{1}{4} + \frac{1}{6} =$

1

Test B: Paper 1 Marks

Q	Question	Possible marks	Actual marks
1	6 + 0.3	1	
2	8 × 3	1	
3	12 + 6 + 9 + 14	1	
4	$\frac{1}{4} + \frac{1}{4} + \frac{1}{4}$	1	
5	1473 − 73	1	
6	25 ÷ 5	1	
7	475 + 98	1	
8	100 × 16	1	
9	2 × 3 × 4	1	
10	1000 ÷ 10	1	
11	$\frac{1}{12} + \frac{10}{12}$	1	
12	1.25 × 10	1	
13	846,248 + 50,000	1	
14	0.77 − 0.25	1	
15	23 × 9	1	
16	0.2 + 0.9	1	
17	$\frac{1}{2}$ of 26	1	
18	387 − 222	1	

Q	Question	Possible marks	Actual marks
19	345 ÷ 100	1	
20	7 + 4 × 6 − 3	1	
21	12,385 + 28,034	1	
22	35 × 40	1	
23	44 × 11	1	
24	1 − 0.65	1	
25	32,406 − 16,273	1	
26	50% of 80	1	
27	$3\overline{)7\ 0\ 4\ 7}$	2	
28	15,634 − 3996	1	
29	87 × 53	2	
30	$\frac{5}{8} - \frac{1}{2}$	1	
31	30 + 3 × 7	1	
32	315 × 34	2	
33	1.75 + 2.16	1	
34	$3 \times 1\frac{1}{2}$	1	
35	$6\overline{)4\ 8\ 2\ 5}$	2	
36	$\frac{1}{3} + \frac{1}{4} + \frac{1}{6}$	1	
	Total	**40**	

Instructions Test B: Paper 2

- You have **40 minutes** for this test paper.
- You may **not use** a calculator to answer any questions in this test paper.
- Work as quickly and carefully as you can.
- Try to answer all the questions. If you cannot do one of the questions, **go on to the next one**. You can come back to it later, if you have time.
- If you finish before the end, **go back and check your work**.
- Ask your teacher if you are not sure what to do.

Follow the instructions for each question carefully.

If you need to do working out, you can use any space on the page – do not use rough paper.

Marks

Some questions have a method box like this.

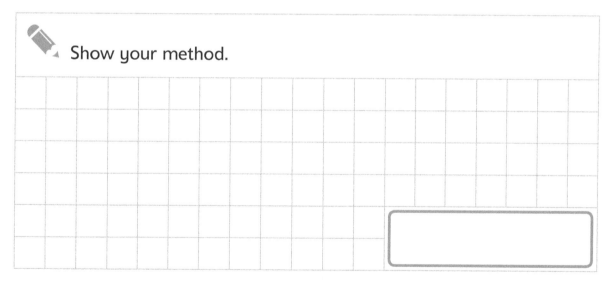

For these questions you may get a mark for showing your method.

The number on the right-hand side of the page tells you the maximum number of marks for each question.

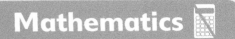
1. What fraction of this square is shaded?

Marks

1

2. Round 23.6 to the nearest whole number.

1

SCHOLASTIC National Curriculum SATs Tests

3. Draw a straight line 53mm long.

Marks

1

4. Complete this sequence.

12,364, 22,364, ☐ , ☐ , ☐ , 62,364

1

5. Write 432,578 in words.

_____

_____

Marks

1

6. 1 inch = 2.54cm

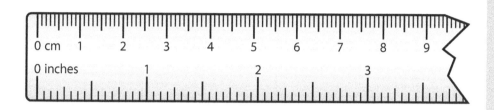

Marks

How many centimetres are there in ten inches?

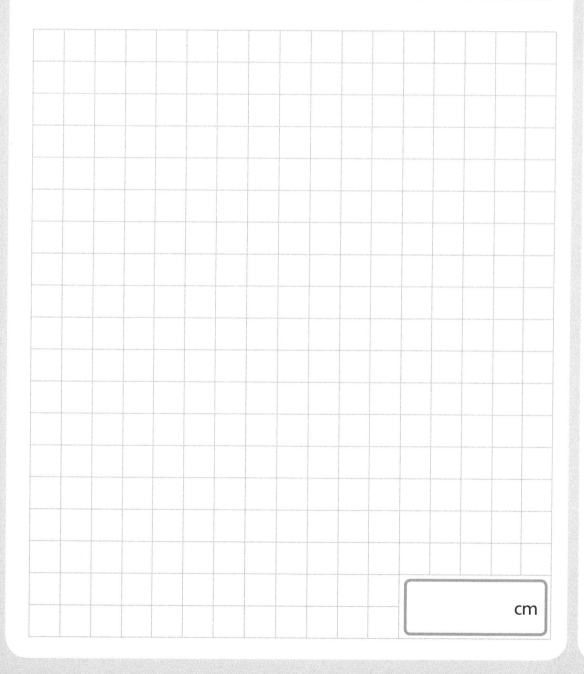

cm

1

7. Write the missing number.

Marks

$$24 \times \boxed{} + 23 = 263$$

1

Marks

8. Write these numbers in order, from smallest to largest.

320,780		945
	89,495	
9759		500,000

1

9. Round each number to the nearest ten thousand.

123,584 ☐

875,000 ☐

1

10. A jug holds 1 litre of water. Each cup holds 120ml.

The jug is full.

Tom fills two cups from the jug.

How much water will be left in the jug?

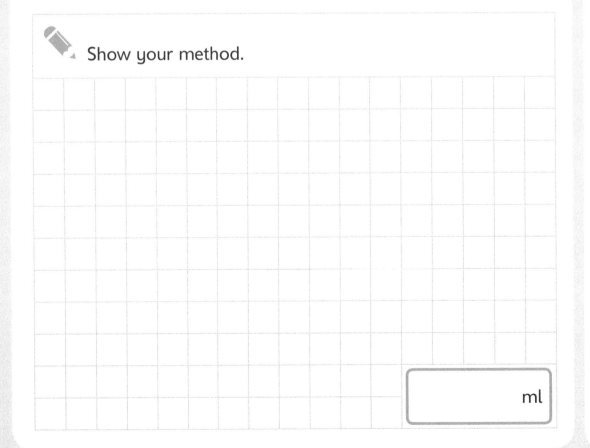

Show your method.

ml

2

SCHOLASTIC National Curriculum SATs Test:

11. Measure each angle below.

Write its size and its name.

Marks

size [   ] °

name [   ]

size [   ] °

name [   ]

2

Marks

12. This data shows the number of children in each year group of a junior school.

Year 3	Year 4	Year 5	Year 6
108	112	119	117

How many children are there in the school altogether?

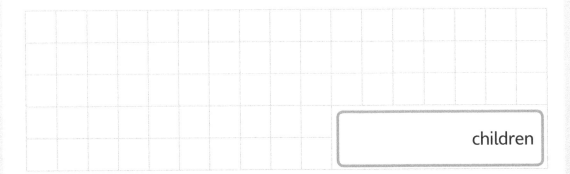

children

1

There are four classes in each year group.

The maximum number of children in each class is 30.

How many spare places are there in the school?

Show your method.

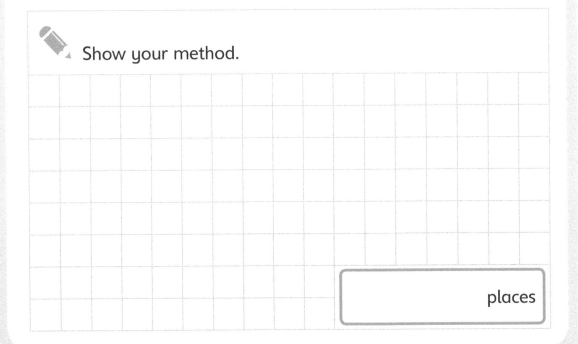

places

2

13. In a library, the shelves can hold 120 books per shelf.

How many books will fit on 20 shelves?

Marks

books

1

14. In a class survey of 36 children, each child was asked which subject they preferred out of English, maths or science.

$\frac{1}{3}$ preferred maths and $\frac{1}{4}$ preferred English.

How many children prefer science?

Marks

✎ Show your method.

children

2

SCHOLASTIC National Curriculum SATs Test

15. If 2½ pizzas are divided equally between 10 children, how much pizza will each child receive?

Marks

✏️ Show your method.

2

Marks

16. A farmer sells eight cows for a total of £6840.

Each cow was sold for the same price.

What was the value of each cow?

🖉 Show your method.

£

2

The farmer uses the money to buy 20 sheep. If there is £40 left over, what was the cost of each sheep?

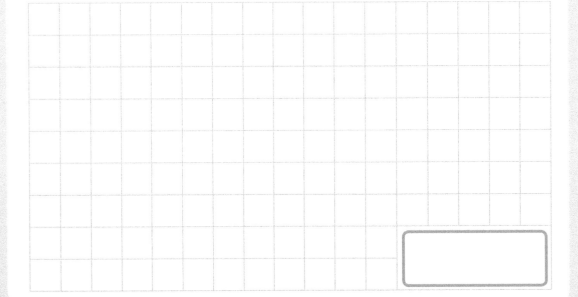

1

SCHOLASTIC National Curriculum SATs Tests

17. Match each definition to the correct quadrilateral. Below each shape, write its name.

Marks

| I have all four sides equal, and opposite angles equal. | I have two pairs of equal sides. They are adjacent to each other. | I only have one pair of parallel sides. |

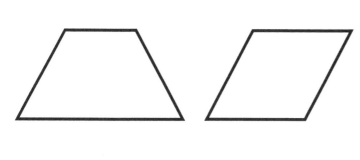 

Name:

2

18. $3\frac{1}{6} + 1\frac{5}{12} + 2\frac{1}{3} =$

Circle the correct answer.

$6\frac{7}{12}$ $6\frac{3}{4}$ $6\frac{11}{12}$ 7

Marks

1

■SCHOLASTIC National Curriculum SATs Test:

Marks

19. A square has a rectangular hole cut out of it. The dimensions of the rectangle are shown below. The diagram is not to scale.

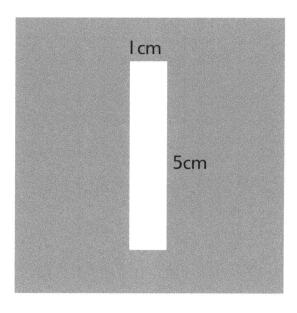

1 cm

5cm

If the shaded area is 31 cm², calculate the length of each side of the square.

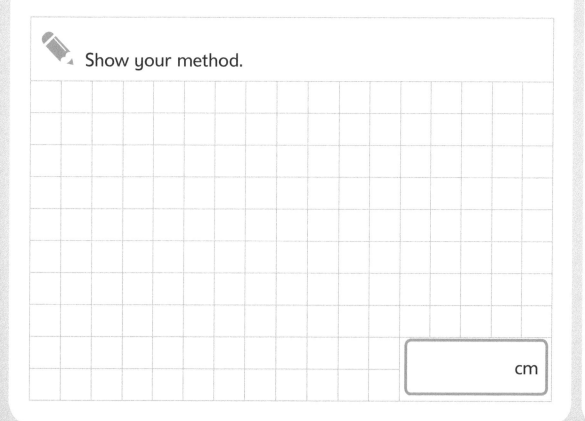

Show your method.

cm

3

20. How many hours are there in a leap year?

Marks

✏ Show your method.

hours

2

SCHOLASTIC National Curriculum SATs Tests

Marks

21. Ben does some shopping.

Here is an incomplete shopping receipt.

Ben paid with a £10 note and received £2.74 change.

Bread:	£1.66
Eggs:	£1.58
Fruit:	£2.53
Milk:	£x.xx

How much did the milk cost?

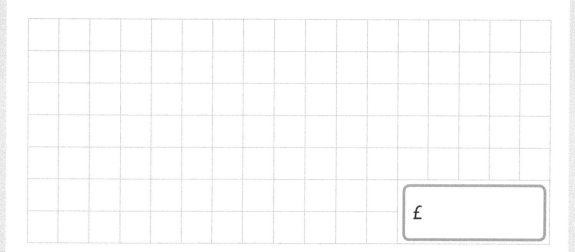

£

1

The shopkeeper needs to order more bread.

She buys items wholesale at half the price she charges her customers.

How much would 120 loaves of bread cost her?

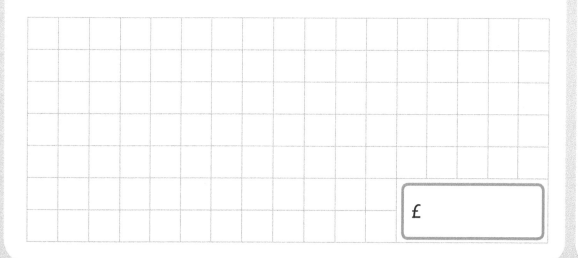

£

1

22. The line graph shows a journey by car.

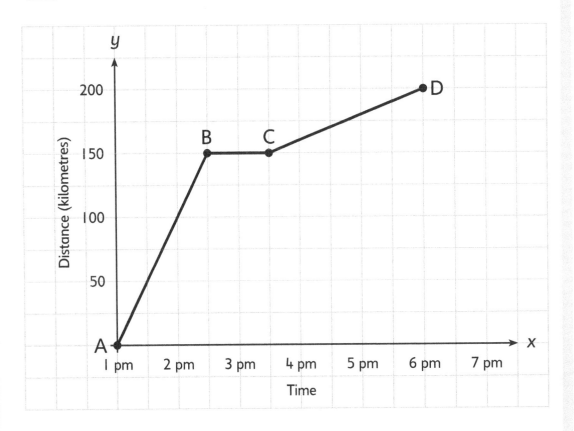

Why is the line horizontal between points B and C?

_____

1

Q	Strand	Sub-strand	Possible marks	Actual marks
1	Fractions, decimals, %	Recognise, find, write, name and count fractions	1	
2	Fractions, decimals, %	Rounding decimals	1	
3	Measurement	Compare, describe and order measures	1	
4	Number and place value	Counting (in multiples)	1	
5	Number and place value	Read, write, order and compare numbers	1	
6	Measurement	Convert between metric units	1	
7	Number and place value	Number problems	1	
8	Number and place value	Read, write, order and compare numbers	1	
9	Number and place value	Identify, represent and estimate; rounding	1	
10	Measurement	Solve problems (capacity)	2	
11	Geometry – properties of shapes	Angles – measuring and properties	2	
12	Calculations	Add / subtract to solve problems	3	
13	Calculations	Multiply / divide mentally	1	
14	Fractions, decimals, %	Multiply / divide fractions	2	
15	Fractions, decimals, %	Solve problems with fractions	2	
16	Calculations	Multiply / divide using written methods	3	
17	Geometry – properties of shapes	Describe properties and classify shapes	2	
18	Fractions, decimals, %	Add / subtract fractions	1	
19	Measurement	Perimeter, area	3	
20	Calculations	Multiply / divide using written methods	2	
21	Measurement	Solve problems (money; length; mass/weight; capacity/volume)	2	
22	Statistics	Solve problems involving data	1	
		Total	**35**	

Instructions Test B: Paper 3

- You have **40 minutes** for this test paper.
- You may **not use** a calculator to answer any questions in this test paper.
- Work as quickly and carefully as you can.
- Try to answer all the questions. If you cannot do one of the questions, **go on to the next one**. You can come back to it later, if you have time.
- If you finish before the end, **go back and check your work**.
- Ask your teacher if you are not sure what to do.

Follow the instructions for each question carefully.

If you need to do working out, you can use any space on the page – do not use rough paper.

Marks

Some questions have a method box like this.

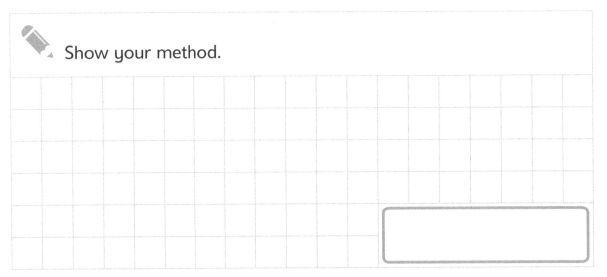

For these questions you may get a mark for showing your method.

The number on the right-hand side of the page tells you the maximum number of marks for each question.

SCHOLASTIC National Curriculum SATs Tests

1. Draw a vertical line to divide this shape into a square and a right-angled triangle.

Marks

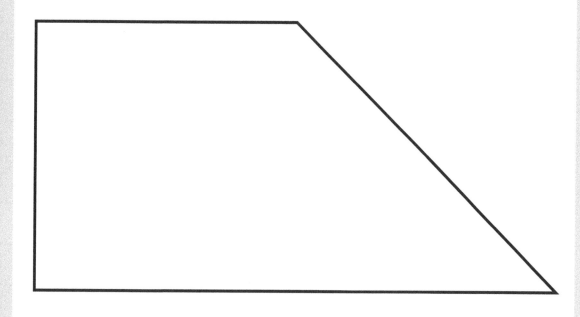

1

2. Write these numbers in order, from smallest to largest.

1705   1507   1057   1075   1570   1750

1

3. Write the two missing digits to make this addition correct.

Marks

$$
\begin{array}{r}
6\ 3\ \boxed{} \\
+\ \boxed{}\ 0\ 9 \\
\hline
9\ 4\ 7
\end{array}
$$

1

4. Complete the chart for each decimal.

Marks

Decimal	Rounded to the nearest whole number	Rounded to one decimal place
0.83		
6.45		
13.5		

2

Marks

5. Insert the correct sign between each pair of fractions, <, > or =.

$$\frac{1}{2} \boxed{} \frac{5}{10} \qquad \frac{1}{4} \boxed{} \frac{3}{8} \qquad \frac{2}{3} \boxed{} \frac{5}{9}$$

1

6. Joanne travels 3 miles to school every day. How far is this in kilometres?

1 mile = 1.61 km

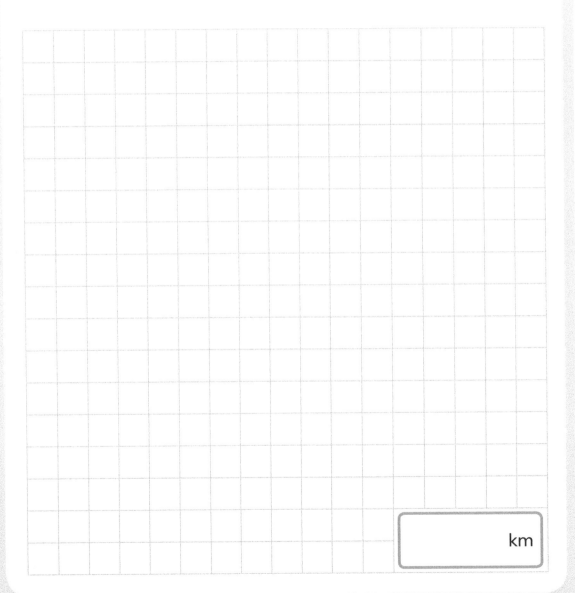

$\boxed{}$ km

1

SCHOLASTIC National Curriculum SATs Tests

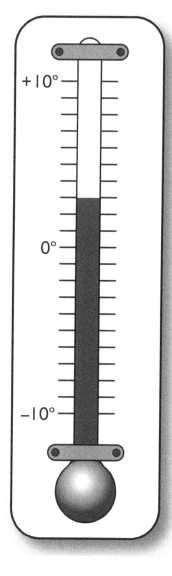
Marks

7. At noon, the temperature in London was 7°C, and the temperature in Moscow was –4°C.

Draw a line and write each city's name next to it on the thermometer.

What is the difference in temperature between Moscow and London?

°C

1

1

Marks

8.   23 children take part in a sports event to raise money for charity.

If every child does 25 star jumps, how many jumps do they do as a whole class?

Show your method.

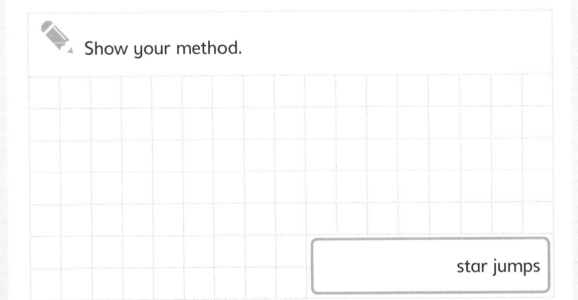

star jumps

2

Joanne's dad says he will give her 5 pence for every star jump she does.

If she does 132 star jumps, how much must her dad pay?

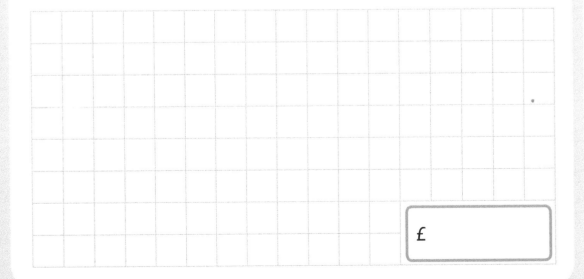

£

1

9. What year do these Roman numerals show?

MMXV

Marks

1

10. Sugar is sold in one kilogram bags.

Rashid uses $\frac{1}{5}$ of a bag of sugar to bake a cake.

How many grams of sugar has Rashid used?

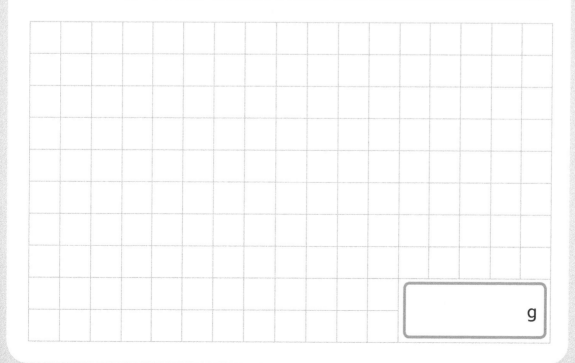

g

1

11. How many ten thousands are there in this number?

536,081

1

12. Triangle 2 is a reflection of triangle 1.

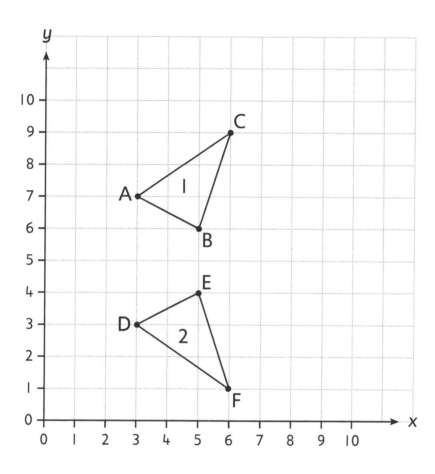

Write the coordinates for each triangle.

Triangle 1: A (___, ___), B (___, ___), C (___, ___)

Triangle 2: D (___, ___), E (___, ___), F (___, ___)

1

Draw the line of reflection (this is sometimes called a mirror line).

1

13. Look at the clock face below. What will the time be in half an hour?

Marks

Write your answer using 12-hour clock time.

1

14. Complete the table to show the properties of these 3D shapes. Write vertically if you need more room.

Marks

Shape				
Name				
Faces				
Edges				
Vertices				

3

15. This is a bus timetable for a small town.

Bus number	5	10	5	10	5	10
Bus station	15:00	15:12	15:30	15:42	16:00	16:12
Primary school	15:08	15:23	15:38	15:53	16:08	16:23
Cinema		15:26		15:56		16:26
Train station	15:15		15:45		16:15	
Doctor's surgery	15:24	15:31	15:54	16:01	16:24	16:31
Train station	15:27	15:34	15:57	16:04	16:27	16:34

Mr Jones has a doctor's appointment at 15:45.

He must catch a bus from the bus station.

Which is the best bus number and time for him to catch so that he is not late but won't have to wait too long?

1

16. Find the only prime number between 90 and 100.

Marks

1

17. Write the missing numbers.

Marks

$$\frac{\boxed{}}{5} \text{ of } 100 = 80$$

1

$$\boxed{} \times 2\frac{2}{3} = 8$$

1

SCHOLASTIC National Curriculum SATs Test

Marks

18. Milo grows a sunflower. The table shows its height, which he has measured once a week for five weeks.

Week	1	2	3	4	5
Height (cm)	2	5	7	9	12

Complete this line graph to show the data.

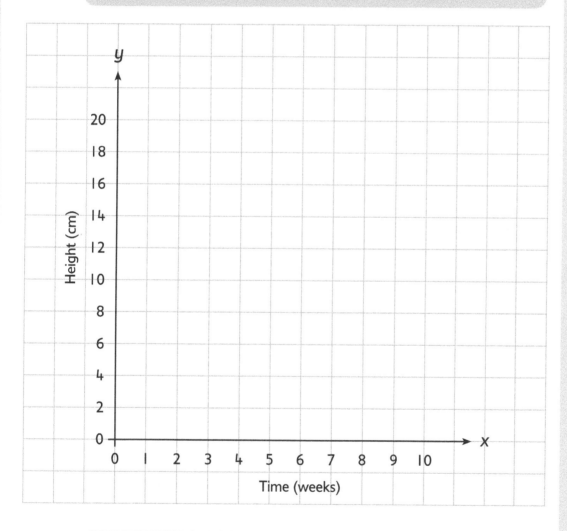

1

Use your graph to predict how high the plant will be after eight weeks.

1

19. Beth swims 30 lengths of a swimming pool.

If the swimming pool is 25 metres long, how many more lengths should she swim to complete 1 km?

Marks

Show your method.

lengths

2

■SCHOLASTIC National Curriculum SATs Tests

Marks

20. Over the summer holidays, Jane's family go on a train tour of Europe. Jane keeps a record of each journey they make.

Journey 1	Journey 2	Journey 3	Journey 4	Journey 5
545 miles	427 miles	604 miles	378 miles	

Jane's ambition is to travel more than 2500 miles in total.

What is the minimum distance they must travel for their last journey for this to happen?

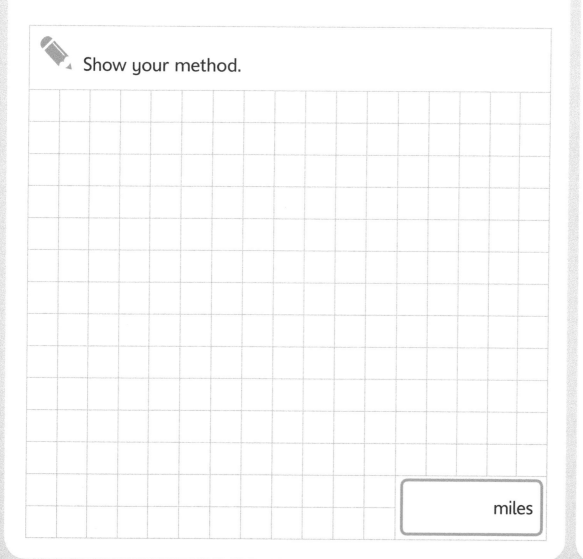

Show your method.

miles

2

Marks

21. Round each of these numbers to the nearest ten thousand and then add them together.

64,523   72,836   51,499

2

SCHOLASTIC National Curriculum SATs Test

22. 120 out of 200 children have blonde hair.

Write this as a percentage.

Marks

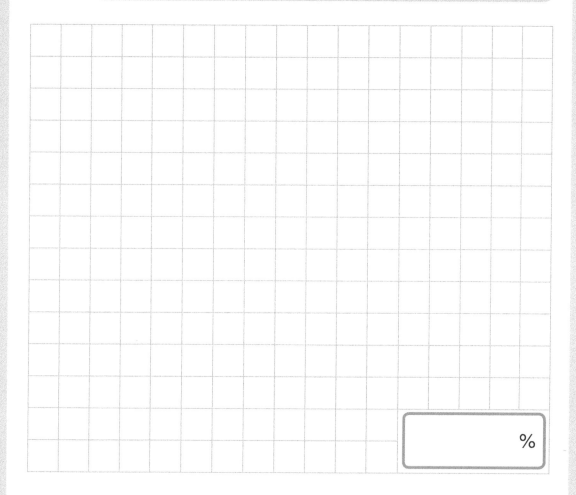

%

1

23. The population of a city is 639,375.

In the summer, many tourists visit and the population grows to 805,648.

How many tourists arrive?

1

Q	Strand	Sub-strand	Possible marks	Actual marks
1	Geometry – properties of shapes	Describe properties and classify shapes	1	
2	Number and place value	Compare and order numbers	1	
3	Calculations	Add / subtract mentally	1	
4	Fractions, decimals, %	Rounding decimals	2	
5	Fractions, decimals, %	Comparing and ordering fractions	1	
6	Measurement	Convert metric/imperial	1	
7	Number and place value	Negative numbers	2	
8	Calculations	Multiply / divide using written methods	3	
9	Number and place value	Place value; Roman numerals	1	
10	Measurement	Solve problems (mass)	1	
11	Number and place value	Place value	1	
12	Geometry – position and direction	Describe position, direction and movement	2	
13	Measurement	Telling time, ordering time, duration and units of time	1	
14	Geometry – properties of shapes	Describe properties and classify shapes	3	
15	Statistics	Interpret and represent data	1	
16	Calculations	Properties of number (primes)	1	
17	Fractions, decimals, %	Multiply / divide fractions	2	
18	Statistics	Solve problems involving data	2	
19	Calculations	Solve problems (commutative, associative, distributive and all four operations)	2	
20	Calculations	Add / subtract to solve problems	2	
21	Number and place value	Number problems (rounding)	2	
22	Fractions, decimals, %	Fractions / decimal / percentage equivalence	1	
23	Calculations	Add / subtract using written methods	1	
		Total	**35**	

Marking and assessing the papers

The mark schemes provide details of correct answers including guidance for questions that have more than one mark.

Interpreting answers

The guidance below should be followed when deciding whether an answer is acceptable or not. As general guidance, answers should be unambiguous.

Problem	Guidance
The answer is equivalent to the one in the mark scheme.	The mark scheme will generally specify which equivalent responses are allowed. If this is not the case, award the mark unless the mark scheme states otherwise. For example: 1 ½ or 1.5
The answer is correct but the wrong working is shown.	A correct response will always be marked as correct.
The correct response has been crossed (or rubbed) out and not replaced.	Do not award the mark(s) for legible crossed-out answers that have not been replaced or that have been replaced by a further incorrect attempt.
The answer has been worked out correctly but an incorrect answer has been written in the answer box.	Where appropriate follow the guidance in the mark scheme. If no guidance is given then: ● award the mark if the incorrect answer is due to a transcription error ● award the mark if there is extra unnecessary workings which do not contradict work already done ● do not award the mark if there is extra unnecessary workings which do contradict work already done.
More than one answer is given.	If all answers are correct (or a range of answers is given, all of which are correct), the mark will be awarded unless specified otherwise by the mark schemes. If both correct and incorrect responses are given, no mark will be awarded.

■ SCHOLASTIC National Curriculum SATs Tests

Problem	Guidance
There appears to be a misread of numbers affecting the working.	In general, the mark should not be awarded. However, in two-mark questions that have a working mark, award one mark if the working is applied correctly using the misread numbers, provided that the misread numbers are comparable in difficulty to the original numbers. For example, if '243' is misread as '234', both numbers may be regarded as comparable in difficulty.
No answer is given in the expected place, but the correct answer is given elsewhere.	Where an understanding of the question has been shown, award the mark. In particular, where a word or number response is expected, a pupil may meet the requirement by annotating a graph or labelling a diagram elsewhere in the question.

Formal written methods

The following guidance, showing examples of formal written methods, is taken directly from the National Curriculum guidelines. These methods may not be used in all schools and any formal written method, which is the preferred method of the school and which gives the correct answer, should be acceptable.

Long multiplication

24 × 16 becomes

```
        2
    2   4
×   1   6
─────────
2   4   0
1   4   4
─────────
3   8   4
─────────
```

Answer: 384

124 × 26 becomes

```
    1   2   4
        ¹   ²
×       2   6
─────────────
2   4   8   0
    7   4   4
─────────────
3   2   2   4
    ¹   ¹
```

Answer: 3224

124 × 26 becomes

```
    1   2   4
        ¹   ²
×       2   6
─────────────
    7   4   4
2   4   8   0
─────────────
3   2   2   4
    ¹   ¹
```

Answer: 3224

Short division

98 ÷ 7 becomes

```
    1   4
  ┌───────
7 │ 9  ²8
```

Answer: 14

432 ÷ 5 becomes

```
        8   6   r2
  ┌───────────────
5 │ 4   3  ³2
```

Answer: 86 remainder 2

496 ÷ 11 becomes

```
         4   5   r1
   ┌───────────────
11 │ 4   9  ⁵6
```

Answer: $45\frac{1}{11}$

Long division

432 ÷ 15 becomes

```
         2   8   r12
   ┌───────────────
15 │ 4   3   2
     3   0   0
   ─────────────
     1   3   2
     1   2   0
   ─────────────
         1   2
```

Answer: 28 remainder 12

432 ÷ 15 becomes

```
         2   8
   ┌───────────────
15 │ 4   3   2
     3   0   0      15 × 20
   ─────────────
     1   3   2
     1   2   0      15 × 8
   ─────────────
         1   2
```

$\frac{12}{15} = \frac{4}{5}$

Answer: $28\frac{4}{5}$

432 ÷ 15 becomes

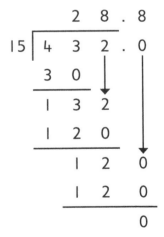

Answer: 28.8

National standard in maths

The mark that each child gets in the test paper will be known as the 'raw score' (for example, '62' in 62/110). The raw score will be converted to a scaled score and children achieving a scaled score of 100 or more will achieve the national standard in that subject. These 'scaled scores' enable results to be reported consistently year-on-year.

The guidance in the table below shows the marks that children need to achieve to reach the national standard. This should be treated as a guide only, as the number of marks may vary. You can also find up-to-date information about scaled scores on our website: www.scholastic.co.uk/nationaltests

Total mark achieved	Standard
0–57	Has not met the national standard in mathematics for Year 5
58–110	Has met the national standard in mathematics for Year 5

Q	Answers	Mark
1	108	1
2	20	1
3	89	1
4	0.2	1
5	44	1
6	870	1
7	9	1
8	104	1
9	96	1
10	$\frac{1}{3}$	1
11	0.9	1
12	25	1
13	30	1
14	564	1
15	$\frac{2}{5}$	1
16	1800	1
17	31	1
18	1008	1
19	855	1
20	23	1
21	20,412	1
22	6.5	1
23	$\frac{3}{4}$	1
24	0.43	1
25	3.2	1
26	124 r2 Award 1 mark for a correct written method for short division but with one arithmetic error.	2
27	6	1
28	7266 Award 1 mark for a correct written method for long multiplication but with one arithmetic error.	2

Q	Answers	Mark
29	71,632	1
30	1050	1
31	8	1
32	16,380 Award 1 mark for a correct written method for long multiplication but with one arithmetic error.	2
33	41	1
34	535 r3 Award 1 mark for a correct written method for short division but with one arithmetic error.	2
35	634.62	1
36	$\frac{1}{2}$ or $\frac{6}{12}$ or $\frac{3}{6}$	1
	Total	**40**

Q	Answers	Marks
1	4 beads should be circled.	1
2	$\begin{array}{r} 4\,\mathbf{5}\,2 \\ -\,1\,2\,\mathbf{0} \\ \hline 3\,3\,2 \end{array}$	1
3	The thermometer should be marked at −5°C (Accept answers that are close, but not if they are ambiguous.)	1
4	1715	1
5	840,000	1
6	3 13 10	1
7	943,506, 944,506, **945,506**, **946,506**, 947,506	1
8	CXXVI	1
9	100,000cm (one hundred thousand) Award 1 mark for correct knowledge of unit conversions. 1m = 100cm and 1km = 1000m	2
10	5440 Award 1 mark for a correct written method but with one arithmetic error.	2
11	Irregular triangle Regular quadrilateral Irregular quadrilateral Regular hexagon 	1
12	<table><tr><th>Fraction</th><th>Decimal</th><th>Percentage</th></tr><tr><td>1/10</td><td>**0.1**</td><td>10%</td></tr><tr><td>1/2</td><td>0.5</td><td>**50%**</td></tr><tr><td>3/4</td><td>**0.75**</td><td>**75%**</td></tr><tr><td>1/1</td><td>1</td><td>100%</td></tr></table>	1

Q	Answers	Marks
13	Yes Award 1 mark for an incorrect answer but with a correct approach to solving the problem and only one arithmetic error.	2
14	28 15 18	1 1 1
15	1 and 24, 2 and 12, 3 and 8, 4 and 6	1
16	2.15pm or 14:15 Accept 14:15pm	1
17	Accept £11,000 or £12,000 or £13,000 £4680 Award 1 mark if the answer is incorrect, but the approach to calculating the answer is appropriate, with a maximum of one arithmetic error in the working.	1 2
18	 A reflected: (4, 8), B reflected: (1, 6), C reflected: (4, 3). Final part must show an understanding that only the x-coordinates change. Accept *The y-coordinates stay the same.*	1 1 1
19	The bar for bus travellers should be 5 units high. The bar should be drawn accurately and to the same width as other bars. Twice as many children *walk* to school than travel by *car*.	1 1

Q	Answers	Marks
20	$\begin{array}{r} 1\ 9\ 3\ 4\ 6 \\ -\ 1\ 2\ 8\ 5\ 7 \\ \hline 6\ 4\ 8\ 9 \end{array}$ or $\begin{array}{r} 1\ 9\ 3\ 4\ 6 \\ -\ \ \ 6\ 4\ 8\ 9 \\ \hline 1\ 2\ 8\ 5\ 7 \end{array}$	1
21	£6.75

Award 1 mark for correct procedure but incorrect answer.
Cost = 75p + 50 × (8p + 2p) = £5.75
Sales = 50 × 25p = £12.50
Profit = sales − cost = incorrect answer | 2 |
| **22** | $\frac{45}{180}$ | 1 |
| **23** | £359

Award 1 mark for a correct written method for short division but with one arithmetic error. | 2 |
| | **Total** | **35** |

■SCHOLASTIC National Curriculum SATs Tests

Q	Answers	Marks
1	Award 1 mark only for all three shapes correctly showing a line of symmetry. The triangle is only symmetrical about a horizontal line.	1
2	Do not award marks for uncertain or ambiguous lines. The line in the answer booklet is 10cm long. Positions on the line should be accurate within 1mm.	1
3	25, 50, 75, **100**, **125**, **150**	1
4	Yes (2480 × 11 = 27,280)	1
5	17°C Do not accept −17.	1
6		1
7	£93.60 Award 1 mark for demonstration of a correct formal method for long multiplication but incorrect answer. 32p per book	2 1
8	Four hundred and sixty-three thousand, nine hundred and one. 704,020	1 1
9	Check that the bar chart has been drawn correctly. Award 1 mark if: ● the bars are all drawn to the correct height ● the bars are of all the same width. $\frac{1}{6}$ of the class have no pet	2 1

Q	Answers	Marks
10	$\frac{1}{12}$ Award 1 mark for correct method to calculate common denominator, with a denominator of 12 found but an incorrect answer.	2
11	279 children	1
12	0.015; 0.051; 0.105; 0.150; 0.501; 0.510	1
13	$45 \div 9 + 53 - 32 = 26$	1
14	270° Reflex angle	1 1
15	LXVII	1
16	£2.50 Award 1 mark for correct approach but wrong answer. Popcorn: £20 − £2 change − ticket prices	2
17	121,929	1
18	3 grapes	1
19	Perimeter = 19m Area = 13.5m² Award 1 mark if the perimeter is correct and the calculation of a single table area is correct. Otherwise award no marks.	2
20	£106,000	1
21	20:00 (accept 8pm, do not accept 9pm or 10pm) 7°C 2.5 hours (accept $2\frac{1}{2}$ hours or 150 minutes)	1 1 1
22	552 people Award 1 mark for 2760 ÷ 2 = 1380 Award 2 marks for 1380 ÷ 5 = 276; 276 × 3 = 828	3
	Total	**35**

Q	Answers	Marks
1	6.3	1
2	24	1
3	41	1
4	$\frac{3}{4}$	1
5	1400	1
6	5	1
7	573	1
8	1600	1
9	24	1
10	100	1
11	$\frac{11}{12}$	1
12	12.5	1
13	896,248	1
14	0.52	1
15	207	1
16	1.1	1
17	13	1
18	165	1
19	3.45	1
20	28	1
21	40,419	1
22	1400	1
23	484	1
24	0.35	1
25	16,133	1
26	40	1
27	2349 Award 1 mark for a correct written method for short division but with one arithmetic error.	2
28	11,638	1

Q	Answers	Marks
29	4611 Award 1 mark for a correct written method for long multiplication but with one arithmetic error.	2
30	$\frac{1}{8}$	1
31	51	1
32	10,710 Award 1 mark for a correct written method for long multiplication but with one arithmetic error.	2
33	3.91	1
34	$4\frac{1}{2}$ or 4.5	1
35	804 r1 Award 1 mark for a correct written method for short division but with one arithmetic error.	2
36	$\frac{9}{12}$ or $\frac{3}{4}$	1
	Total	**40**

■SCHOLASTIC National Curriculum SATs Test

Q	Answers	Marks
1	$\frac{1}{8}$	1
2	24	1
3	Ensure line is 53mm. It should be drawn with a ruler and accurate to within 1mm.	1
4	12,364, 22,364, **32,364**, **42,364**, **52,364**, 62,364	1
5	Four hundred and thirty-two thousand, five hundred and seventy-eight.	1
6	25.4cm	1
7	10	1
8	945 9759 89,495 320,780 500,000	1
9	120,000 880,000	1
10	760ml Award 1 mark for a correct written method but with one arithmetic error.	2
11	90°, right angle 165°, obtuse angle (Allow inaccuracies within 1°) Award 1 mark for each angle measured and named correctly. Award 1 mark if both angles are measured correctly but named incorrectly, or vice versa.	2
12	456 children 24 spare places If the second answer is incorrect, award 1 mark for a method which shows a clear understanding of the appropriate order of procedures. For example, calculate year group 4 × 30 = 120 calculate school capacity 4 × 120 = 480 subtract current number 480 − 456 = incorrect answer	1 2
13	2400 books	1
14	15 children Award 1 mark for a correct written method but with one arithmetic error.	2

Q	Answers	Marks
15	$\frac{1}{4}$ pizza each. Award I mark for correctly identifying $2\frac{1}{2} = \frac{1}{2}$ children.	2
16	£855 Award I mark for correct formal written method for short division but with one arithmetic error. £340	2 1

17 (2 marks)

I have all four sides equal, and opposite angles equal.

I have two pairs of equal sides. They are adjacent to each other.

I only have one pair of parallel sides.

Trapezium   Rhombus   Kite

Q	Answers	Marks
18	$6\frac{11}{12}$	1
19	Side length of square = 6cm Award 2 marks for the correct calculation but an incorrect arithmetic error. $1 \times 5 = 5 + 31 = 36\text{cm}^2 =$ total area area = $a \times b$ for square = $a \times a$ $a \times a$ = incorrect answer Award I mark for working out the correct total area and attempting to work out the perimeter.	3
20	8784 hours Award I mark for a correct written method for long multiplication but with one arithmetic error.	2
21	£1.49 £99.60	1 1
22	The car is not moving; it has stopped.	1
	Total	**35**

SCHOLASTIC National Curriculum SATs Tests

Q	Answers	Marks
1	 (Line should be accurate within 1mm.)	1
2	1057 1075 1507 1570 1705 1750	1
3	$\begin{array}{r} 6\,3\,8 \\ +\,3\,0\,9 \\ \hline 9\,4\,7 \end{array}$	1

4 (2 marks)

Decimal	Rounded to the nearest whole	Rounded to one decimal place
0.83	1	0.8
6.45	6	6.5
13.50	14	13.5

Award 1 mark for at least four correct answers.

Q	Answers	Marks
5	$\frac{1}{2}=\frac{5}{10}$, $\frac{1}{4}<\frac{3}{8}$, $\frac{2}{3}>\frac{5}{9}$	1
6	4.83km	1
7	Marks on thermometer should be accurate to within 1mm on the scale provided, Moscow at −4°C and London at +7°C.	1
	11°C	1
8	575 star jumps Award 1 mark for a correct written method but with one arithmetic error. £6.60	2 1
9	2015	1
10	200g	1
11	Accept 3 or three	1

Q	Answers	Marks
12	Triangle 1: A(3, 7), B(5, 6), C(6, 9) Triangle 2: D(3, 3), E(5, 4), F(6, 1) (Do not award mark if any coordinates are incorrect.)	1
	Horizontal line at $y = 5$ (Do not award marks for ambiguous lines or more than one line.)	1
13	Ten past six Accept 6:10am, 6:10pm or 6:10	1
14		3

Shape				
Name	cube	cone	cylinder	triangular prism
Faces	6	2	3	5
Edges	12	1	2	9
Vertices	8	0	0	6

Award 2 marks if all shapes are named correctly and three of the shapes have all properties correct.

Award 1 mark if all shapes are named correctly but other information is incorrect.

Q	Answers	Marks
15	The number 10 bus at 15:12. (Do not accept just the bus number.)	1
16	97	1
17	4	1
	3	1
18	Graph should show all points accurately marked with a small cross, with individual points connected by straight lines.	1
	Accept any estimated height between 17cm and 20cm. The graph does not have to be marked to show this, but mark as correct if it is and the answer box is blank.	1
19	10 lengths	2
	Award 1 mark for working out the distance. $30 \times 25 = 750 - 100 = 250$	

Q	Answers	Marks
20	546 miles Award 1 mark for a correct addition of the four distances shown (1954 miles)	2
21	60,000 + 70,000 + 50,000 = 180,000 Award 1 mark for all numbers rounded correctly. Award 1 mark for a correct addition of rounded numbers.	2
22	60%	1
23	166,273	1
	Total	**35**